M000202086

I wrote this as an attempt to understand myself and as a gift to those who still love me. Miller McKenzie is no one.

Part 1 of 2

I'm just terrified, so so terrified to be whoever I am, because it's not who I know, it's so new, and lonely, this is what no one talks about, no one tells you that on the other side of healing awaits a stranger. A stranger that you have to live with, a stranger that you have to feed, a stranger you have to make coffee for, and walk in the afternoons with. A stranger you have to care for in a way you never have, a stranger that deserves more love than you've ever known how to give, I'm scared of this stranger, I'm so terrified of breaking the heart of whoever I become.

I have scrapped myself out and reminded myself that even cacti can flower.

I'm in a beautiful wasteland being recycled. I am being repurposed, and the machines have been crushing me. I hope the paint brushes hurt less. I hope the delivery driver leaves me in a safe place when I arrive. I hope my heart pumps softly into the world from then on.

Heaven is full of echidnas and platypuses, fairy bread and baby's breath.

The water lay down in front of me, waiting to be tucked in to bed by the blanket that is the night sky. The sun and I were reading a book to the waves. The golden light bounced over the faces of the ocean until the chapter had come to an end.

Everything was still, and for the first time that day, I could see the sun without her hurting my eyes. She looked at me and sighed. I sat there crying.

Me and the sun both waved goodbye to each other knowing this was all we were. A series of goodbyes. There was no way I would be up in the morning to say hello. Not any day soon, not tomorrow. Though the sun does throw rocks at my window at the earliest possible moment. She knows I want to sleep through the racket of life.

It's terribly unfair to have to do your best while at your worst.

My heart always goes where it's not wanted. It stands in the corner watching on as the one it wants dances and kisses another.

Forgiveness is ripping out a weed from inside your heart and planting a sunflower there instead.

Every mistake I've made in my life so far feels like each was a log being thrown onto a fire. So many logs now crackling under my ribs burning me from the inside. I wait for the day a flame bursts out of my belly button.

And when I sit on the end of my bed I feel as though the hands of life are constantly behind me, ready to touch my shoulders simultaneously to give me another fright so big that it leaves a shadow I can see even when I am in the dark.

But when I am on the cliffs, that is a place where no hands can touch me.

When I see photographs of you and me, I see two people who don't exist anymore. But I know the new versions of us would do better, I know the versions of us that made it past the unanswered questions would be more kind. I know this because in me there's an old version missing you so badly. It's okay though, the old version is a bit silly, the old version can't see that the new version of me grew from an old version of you.

And sometimes you can't tell whether you are crying in the snow or crying at the snow. And sometimes you are shaking like a leaf, and sometimes you can remember figuring a love heart with your index finger on the car window from the internal heat.

Give me a funeral even though I am not dead.
I'm a new born in a new world.
Eyes are a banana.
I am new born. I am peeled, I am peeled.

# Autonomous Sun On The Platypus River

I start burning under the same sun everyone else burns under, the same sun everyone who's ever been looks to and burns under. I am so small, so small and burnt. I walk on, missing everyone but walking further and further away from anyone. I walk on, burning and missing, sobbing and laughing, if I could do this forever maybe I would. I step in mud, my shin slides in like a knife through a chocolate cake, I don't miss the smell of coffee anymore.

Everyone really just wants to make a home inside the heart of someone they know loves them. That's the universal want of the world. We all just want to put monsteras in the aorta of a chest with perfect sunlight and enough water.

I don't know if glow worms know that they glow the way they do, and I don't know if humans do either.

Little lights we are.

There were many broken trees and even a snake or two on the track today. This often-walked track, this often-seen, often-heard and often-smelt, dirt carpet that spends its days slithering through the wattle.

I stepped off it and ventured away toward the dolerite cliffs, toward the beauty only those who have things forcing them off their tracks get to see. I became part of the seldom, as I was leaving the often behind.

The horizon had three rainbows on it, only because I wanted it that way.

I've spent more days laying down this year than I have standing up, and my back and heart are both sore.

I feel like I'm slowly learning to become a sun, I have spent my life as a moon, I have spent my life needing someone else's light to shine, but I can feel a glow inside of me now.

My brain has melted together some strange combination of hope and regret. I don't know when or if I will adjust to a lonely disconnected life, some days it's bearable and some it is not. I feel like I could meet a thousand new people in the next year and it wouldn't be enough to fill the you sized hole in me that I am missing.

I want to have a child, but I'm scared it would inherent the thoughts I have had to endure throughout my life.

I hate experiencing the world without you. I want to show you what I've found.

It's been 4 days since the mountain disappeared behind the weather, a grey cloud stands in the way of my only friend in this small city, I feel extra lonely when I can't see the mountain, I feel my life has less purpose when I can't check for snow on the cap.

And when they come to cross the bridges that broke their hearts, they will see me standing on the railing, waiting to be talked down.

It appears that I am no longer needed. It appears I cannot be used anymore. It appears I have been switched off, that someone's taken the batteries out. Like an annoying clock in a hotel room with floral curtains, I'm on my side, breathing in and out, not making a sound, not needed.

I'm reaching out my fingertips, and that's when I feel a clinched fist hit my face, it hurts like a kiss.

Often times on my walks at dusk my eyes are watering, and often times I cannot tell whether that's because of the cold air or my broken leaky head.

I wonder if the space you took up in my heart was equal to the space, I took up in yours.

# Autonomous Sun On The Platypus River

The voices in my head
are angels telling me to sleep.

I feel like all the pieces of my heart I gave to everyone so willingly and carelessly are now gone forever.

I used to be able to feel myself in the hearts of others but now I don't, I don't feel myself in anything.

If dead trees are beautiful so are dead memories.

I want love to feel like the way Jose Gonzalez plays heartbeats.

Everyone but me could see the broken state I had lived my life in. I was always trying to heal and be better and see for myself the brokenness. But as humans do, I struggled, I failed, I caught glimpses, but rubbed my eyes so many times that I blurred my vision as I looked in the mirror. Denial crept inside me and made itself comfortable in my loving and good heart, denial was hugging good intent so tightly that I couldn't see the incompleteness and lack of self, inside of me. But I see now, because tragedy, loss, grief and pain have washed my eyes clear, and the denial of being broken is no longer present. I am in pieces now, 1000 paper puzzle cut outs poured onto the table, cardboard side up, I can tell from the box that when I'm done, beauty will be there to see and feel. I believe in who I can be, I believe that who I can be was who I always wanted to be and was always there within me.

I miss meeting everyone I've ever loved in the corner of parties I didn't want to be at.

It was always so noisy and quiet all at once with you. I could hear the cicadas singing constantly whenever we went and laid in the sun. I felt every fly land on the hairs of my legs, and I could always feel you. Until one day I couldn't. Until one day the cicadas stopped their song, and the sun was smothered in clouds. And it rained for months from my eyes.

So many stops on the side of the road, so much beauty on the roads, you just have to stop. Maybe that was my problem, or where it went wrong, I only stopped to piss and eat, that's all I ever did. I'm sorry I didn't stop to love you more.

The hotel was all off cream coloured, it was nauseating, you were angry, and I knew you didn't love me anymore.

And so, I am stuck in a fairy tale, my legs are a fable, holding me up as I look down a never-ending road, no signs, no lights, no reflection, no ends, no means, just stars, and my bag that I stuffed full of beans and dreams.

We had everything we could ever want, at least for where we were. Cocaine, alcohol, tension, secrets, a bathroom, friendship, plants, a light, phones, money, love, hate, anxiety, depression, happiness, sadness. We were hopeless but we were sure of ourselves, we were confident, we liked ourselves and each other for fifteen minutes. We loved who we were when we were the types who others would see as people making a memory.

We loved who we were most when we pretended not to care about tomorrow.

Boy of my mind, frantic and sunburnt,
anxiety arises, there's a blemish inside.
No skincare routine can wipe a smile.
As those who lost, laugh and vomit.
As those who came, stop and stare.
Boy of my mind, who I want to be,
city lights illuminate me, red and green,
let's pick a Christmas tree.

Set it up in the corner of your room,
buy yourself a gift, give yourself a seed.
Water it and watch it bloom, let it be
everything you need.

Let it be everything you need.

Fall into a pattern, swim inside a wave, fall asleep in the
mouth of a cave.

You have to stop calling those who have never answered you, because sometimes giving up is the only way out of the pain.

She fell out of love and on that day the bird nest outside his window grew legs and jumped from the tree. The eggs cracked on the ground, and waited for the rain to clean up the brokenness below.

A sneezing man watched it all as he waited for the train, the sky was on fire, bumble bees meandered on the flowers above, but she was out of love, she was gone, so she will never know.

As I write my story, I am reminded that everyone else is writing theirs, and in some of those I am the villain. So sometimes we just have to accept no matter how hard we try, no matter how much good we attempt, we will always be the villain of someone's story, if that's the way they want to write it.

You can't control anyone else's narrative.

It's as though I was destined to miss only the people who don't miss me.

The world ripped me open and showed me what was inside. I wasn't happy with the way they opened me, so many cuts, so many bruises, but if they had never done so, I wouldn't be aware of the rot. The parts that went bad, the spread of ill will.

The gunk of the past is in buckets now, stored in the back, it's not something you can pour down the sink or flush down the toilet, you got to keep your gunk, you have to know and remember what you can create when you aren't paying attention to who you are becoming.

And I can still feel your knee touching mine while I watch movies alone in the cinema so big, so big.

Drop me between mountains and leave me there, I won't
rot.

My pack is to the brim with white flags, I'll hand them all out when I'm done, I need to surrender this life.

I didn't want to be at the end, I tried to write more, tried to find a way to begin again.

Me and the Pink Robin sit and drink tea as we paused time together. Never to reset it ever again.

It's so easy to stay inside, to stay in bed. Hiking is uncomfortable, but that is how you grow and so I drag my feet out to the trails, and I stomp a print on the hillsides and fall into puddles of mud, and wade through water and cry under the stars and I grow bigger and bigger and bigger, and my heart grows fuller and fuller and fuller.

My heart is so broken that I have had to start pumping a new one.

Day one, I am not sore but I am lonely.

Day six, I am sore but I am not lonely.

I went outside in the wild to go inside of myself.

Everyone on the trail is walking off some kind of pain, whether they know it or not, every step is a sip from the cup that is natures healing. And I came to drink.

Some of my best memories are with people who hurt me in ways that changed my life forever and that is why my window is always crying.

I wish you were here now. I wish I hadn't met you; I mean I wish I was yet to meet you; I wish we were meeting tomorrow for the first time, or next week, or even last Thursday would have been okay, but not 16 years ago, not then.

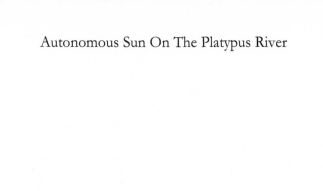

Autonomous Sun On The Platypus River

You can show me your bruises and I'll see you again tomorrow and tomorrow and tomorrow and tomorrow.

Pages of my book were ripped out and fed to the family dog.

And now I have to shout even louder to be heard, I have to stand even taller to be seen, and I have to love even deeper to exist.

# Autonomous Sun On The Platypus River

A pink and white dream is pulling me apart
while cherry blossom petals are falling in my heart.

Will I always break the arms that try to hold me, including my own?

I am so cold.

The monster wasn't inside of me anymore
It was stuck in my shadow. And I'll always be scared to
walk in the sun because of it.

I told him who I used to be; he didn't flinch. I told him I was horrible.

Dear God.

I hope one day to return to child, to be who I was before pain, to be a stranger to the world. To be best friends with lady bugs and have dreams of becoming an astronaut.

I have it all figured out, I'm going to be no one and do nothing.

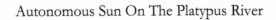

We all have to let go of the things that broke us, even if they rip out parts of you as you wave goodbye to them.

I feel heavy with the memory of how I became a person I could have never loved.

# Autonomous Sun On The Platypus River

And we both got our hands on ropes, hoisting up the times of our life, smoking on the balcony under a million stars in the snow, blankets and a guitar, music on the PlayStation, eighteen years old and no mistakes made so far, complaining about a life that was perfect.

I'm cursed by the man I have been, isn't everyone though? Yellow and pretty like lemon, sour sour and seed filled, nowhere to plant for this future spell casting, broken magician, baby star humanoid, weeping onto a teabag left in the sink. Staining, staining memorabilia of those who are kitchen weak.

Some days I get questions from life and others I get answers, though recently it's been a lot of questions. I drink three litres of water and make my bed at least twice a week in hope of finding the next day of answers.

Someone who lives in the world knows more than someone who reads about how to.

I suppose it is a conversation of which we must try and decipher when no one else is around, the sound of water in a bay on a tiny white sand beach. Lapping always lapping, like a cat tongue in a ceramic bowl of milk, if we contain multitudes so then too does the water in which we swim.

If Kerouac can transcribe what the sea said then I can surely listen and hear the pain of the mountains. Who to everyone else are beautiful but to themselves are just rocks stuck in limbo, wedged in time, and for some I have heard, a time they didn't want to be stuck in. "I had more growing to do" said one, "I was hoping more trees would settle on me but I was too ambitious when I was young, I shot so high that nothing can live on me, no life just snow, just cold fucking snow" said another. "I am not a mountain though" shouted the hill, jealous but beautiful.

Poor jellyfish.

Everything you ever got so worked up over, excitedly so or hatefully filled, will either die when you do, having held your mind captive your whole life and be in the memory of no one else, and reveal itself as utterly pointless clutter to your heart. Or it can be thrown out right now, as you drink coffee, read books and walk nature, leaving your thoughts bathed, smelling good, and smiling at the black inner walls of your skull, the home of unnecessary troubles.

The most reoccurring feeling I've had throughout my life is that wherever I am, someone doesn't want me to be there. So, I hope one day as I keep moving forward in my life, I can find a place that hugs me as I enter it, and fights to keep me when I try to leave.

Once you learn how to find your way in the dark, moving in the light is easy.

Woke up with pains all over, outside and in, pains in my lower back and an itch on my heart. Naked and cold, got my shoulder out the blanket, oh well I guess it's time to get up, pour some blueberries into my mouth, wash my cold shoulder with hot water downstairs.

Chipping away at the books on the shelf, reading them all together as if they were one, the greatest story ever told or a bad idea that's only making me dumb, remember the time the rainbow of light hit the corner chair in our lounge room due to the perfectly accurate sun?

Spindle, on your face down the back in the pines, the always on time sun in the sky, warming your cold shoulders without me around, lightning boy bouncing in the sky, it's okay, when it rains, I live in your eye. Rare and rare and always know there's at least one spare, always one heart spare.

Its 4.08am, I just stood in my kitchen eating a chocolate cake, alone, naked, cold, but comfortable. Life seems to be rocking me to death like a baby going to sleep in the arms of a mother, slow and calm. I've got cream all through my moustache and chocolate in my teeth, laughing in the mirror, maybe I will just skip sleeping all together tonight, I really wish I could, it's my only chance at seeing the sunrise.

We ask so much of the people around us purely so they can meet our comfort levels. Though we embrace the uncomfortableness of nature and its unpredictably wild comings and goings. But we really do hate when humans try replicate the same freedom of which the wind howls to. We really are quite stupid and unfair with each other.

I can feel the old bad parts of me slowly shutting down, punching their clocks for the last time.

You start wondering is there any sunlight kind enough to shine without leaving a burn.

I remember you smiling and laughing, smoking cigarettes on an old couch around a fire in the backyard of a party we made up for ourselves.

It isn't the lost that seek god, it's the found.

Life is so still when I look outside late at night, and yet I am filled with this overwhelming anxiety as if what I am looking outside into is a tsunami, and not just empty air and tungsten lights.

If you are going to bottle your emotions, do so in a terrarium.

You will make big mistakes, but it's okay.

You are allowed to go wrong by accident or due to lack of guidance and or maturation because you have a history that taught you to survive rather than grow. You are allowed to go wrong unknowingly or recklessly to know how to go right on purpose, brilliantly, as you walk into the shortbread filled afternoons of your future laughing with new friends, petting the dog of your dreams.

I want you to forgive me, not because I need your forgiveness, but because I want you to be free from hatred and the traps of resentment and bitterness. I want to stop your ankles from bleeding, I want peacocks to sleep on the edge of your nose, I want beauty to be forever in front of you.

I'm so conditioned to hear goodbyes, so good at them, that when you came, I never heard you say hello. I never saw that you were coming to stay, not just passing through like the rest. So, I'm sorry, but would you like a biscuit and what side of the bed do you prefer to sleep on?

I'm not suicidal, but I've wanted to and wished I would die. My cup is half full, it's a gross cocktail of life ending wishes and childlike hope, it's a murky drink, it tastes bad and has for some time. Some stupid humanity left inside of me believes there are ingredients in this world to make my cup taste good again, and so with pain and optimism folded into my pockets, I move. Resisting the urge to pour my drink down the drain.

Closure can't be relied on to heal you, only acceptance can.

You have to keep going, because if you don't you will no longer see life, you will no longer see people smiling and laughing, you won't see a baby stop crying as soon as its mother holds it, you have to keep going so you don't miss the sun falling out of the sky dragging a golden paint brush down the back of all the trees and houses in your town.

Tonight, the worm that has been for so long- digging inside my head, finally found a place it could hurt me from. It's eating, and I can feel it, it's chewing on my laughter, and nibbling my smiles. There's a worm in my brain killing me as slowly as the travels of snails. With every bite the worm enters new words to my thoughts, like a finger punching letters on a type writer. Crunch, how, crunch, do, crunch, I, crunch, go on?

And the wars are all new now, they are fought between you and me and me and me, everyday inside our heads, outside the shops, beside the fountain in the parks, we almost got our wings, let's ruin the statues.

When there is no sun, sunflowers look to face each other,
I miss being able to face you.

Everything burns in the fire, so be careful what you leave in the flames, some will make smoke that makes choke our little neck holes, while others will see cupcake sized memories dancing between the twiglets. Fairy bread embers for breakfast, bread filled with woodgrains, a life once loved in the dirt, lost bracelet, human made paper chain.

Your presence in my life is like a little lighthouse. Your light spins around, though it spins super slowly, and I don't always feel like I'm in it, I always know it's coming back to hit me in time, and I live for those days when I'm standing in the beams of you, little lighthouse.

I'll come home eventually, maybe with hair dye on my head, pink or blue, blonde or black, nose pierced, 10kg heavier, talking about a life lived alone, no one will care for my stories but will nod and smile regardless. Because that's what people do, nod and smile while wishing you'd shut up being angry at you when you don't.

Some people say that all wounds will heal, but I am not sure, so far, healing has just been bleeding. It took me so long to even know what was causing my pain, life stuck a sword in me long ago, slid it through my back and had it carve up and inside my rib cage underneath my heart.

I felt it always, but I couldn't see it, I knew what it was, I knew because it cut those who got close to me, they'd come in for a hug and be sliced by the blade sticking out of my body, a blade I couldn't even see.

Something makes me wonder if they could see it though, and they chose to take the cut, out of love or stupidity or both.

I don't know anymore, but I do know now that it's gone, and has been for some time.

I've been bleeding ever since; I ask myself where is time? Where are you to stop my bleeding, I've put band aids and bandages on over the years but the blood still comes. At one point I stitched it up, this great big gash, hoping it would hold, while waiting for time.

One morning I woke up and stretched so hard that the stitches exploded open and I was bleeding all over again, I collapsed back into my bed and didn't wake up again for 6 more months, I was of course covered in blood. Where is time?

I was born with a broken heart, weren't you?

If you can't miss what it is you never knew then why is it that I do, I do.

People seem to only care and talk about depression when it's visible and manifests in a visceral way like alcohol or drug abuse, cutting, eating disorders, or uncontrollable emotional swings.

No one really ever talks about depression in the way that most people experience it, the depression that soaks into your bed and covers you in a weight so heavy you feel as though you can never lift it. Not only that, it forces a voice inside of you to tell you that you don't even want to lift it. That there is no point in trying to lift it.

So, you just lay there, with nothing, wanting nothing, dreaming of nothing, remembering nothing, becoming nothing.

It's silent, yet excruciatingly loud, it feels like the universe is screaming whispers in your ears.

Your life changes most when you realise you were born to implode into disaster and that not just you were born to do this but everyone else was too.

We were running red lights on the way to the big game, my hand on the hook above the window, when you hit the corners too fast, laughing at me being a nervous passenger.

How is it that you think I can be evil, but that you are only flawed?

The sand is cold on my back and I can feel it right through three layers, it reminds me of when I was homeless fifteen years ago sleeping on the beach. I'm here under the stars, re-memorising my life, in 15 years I want to remember the cold sand under the burning light, travelling death beam filled sky that I love to be beneath, In the inlet, beside the trees, with the sound of water trying to untie my shoes and introduce me to seahorses.

I've never been running from; I am always running to.

Many people are more broken than you'd know, simply because they've found a way to seal the cracks, they've shoved something in to stop the leak. But like a shattered plate that's been glued back together, whether the person who is looking can see it or not, there are pieces no longer whole in all of us.

I hope you get to hear how much I loved being there, in our home, cleaning schedules and cooking goats cheese, run out of space, run out of plates, run out of time, we can't ever die while we draw squiggly sand lines, hoping one day we cross them at the same time.

There's no room anymore for me, so I'll take myself out the back of the bar on a horse heading for the cliffs. I'll be sipping my whiskey while keeping my secrets close to my heart, I'll be keeping it to myself that I'm riding on a Pegasus. Rainbow road waits for me, tiny monsters in my mouth, dreams in a capsule, seems that I've lost the actual, of life, but I'm swimming good beneath a tornado sky.

Last night I reached out to all of my friends, no one reached back. I then reached out to god, I heard a beep and was asked to leave a message.

Beer is too damn depressing, it's delicious but it makes me
so sad. I'm not a drunk, I've barely drank enough in 3 years
to be drunk let alone be a drunk. Every beer I have though
reminds me of all the sadness I wiped off onto leaves and
rocks as I walked trails trying to forget my life.

I can't enjoy things without thinking so much about why I shouldn't be enjoying them. I hate myself while doing nothing but I hate myself even more when I do things.

Nothing scares me more than the thoughts in my head on the bad days.

I wish we talked more about God, and I wish we bought a bird of paradise or two.

What was I supposed to do with all the fear inside of me, what do I do with all the fear seeping still? Shame doesn't scar, it haunts, and drips, and stalks, and hunts, and kills.

I want to be loved ordinarily, I wish I knew how to make coffee, and had nice enough teeth to smile at people properly, I love when people make my coffee well and smile at me properly.

Witnessing you is like looking inside an immortal heart born millions of years ago, that bleeds only love to those who come and that has millions more years of bleeding love to give.

I have dreams sometimes that you are hearing me out, that we are friends again, which I guess in some ways are nightmares to wake up from.

If I could choose my dreams every night, I'd put you in all of them, but I can't, though I do choose my life, so I will put you in all of it and make sure that when you are cold… No, actually forget that! I'll make sure you are never cold, I'll make sure you are always warm, I'll make sure that I buy clothes that have pockets that are always big enough to fit both of our hands in. I will make sure we own blankets that have the weight of a person built into them for the times I am away, 90kg of goose feathers! We will get a dog that smells good, and has soft hair. I want to keep you always warm, like a bath that never needs topping up with hot water.

Why can't I just go to sleep when I am sick of being awake!

I think the memories of the people we have lost are like photos, as long as we keep an album inside of us then the person you loved is alive forever. Sadly, it seems my heart has been filling up with urns, full of ashes, burnt photos, bridges, skin, life.

Attention was brought to everything that I was, it allowed me for the first time to be able to then accept those things and then from that place, actually change.

You can't change if you don't know what you are working on.

You can't put bus tires on a car.

Always be a flower.

If you aren't trying to understand, you are always going to be on the wrong side.

We are in each other's prayers and I've learned it's better to be there than nowhere.

All my yesterday's became reasons to pour beauty into my tomorrow's, which makes my today's worth living.

Life was moving in and out of the shadows of the cafe, people lazing on old chairs drinking coffee, laughing and gossiping. Babies giggling and screaming all in the one breath, life was moving in and out of me, and so I returned to sit in the sunlight like a bear after a long winters rest, who's afraid to see me? Who thinks I'm nice? The coffee is perfect, and the toasted sandwiches made me appreciate pickled mustard again.

I pictured my life before me, constantly forgetting items on a shopping list I wouldn't have ever wanted to write. I pictured my life constantly forgetting my friend's birthdays, but always being the best gift giver whenever I did remember. I pictured my life where the bread was always eaten the day it was bought, where the cheese was locally made. I pictured my life and saw my wife dancing in the kitchen in a yellow dress that bounced off the back of her ankles as she turned laughing and singing. I pictured tiny footsteps trailing mud over the floorboards and saw tiny hand marks on the walls, I pictured paint everywhere and flowers never dying. I pictured my life and saw myself always dressed perfectly for whatever the temperature outside was. I was crying myself to sleep, forgetting the bills piled in the draw beneath the sink, I pictured my life as my future and not my dream.

The steam from her mug swallowed the bottom half of the window. She drew a kitten's face with her finger which made the birds fly away and made her collapse into a tiny ball of laughter.

I was by the stove burning the eggs because I couldn't stop looking at her nose as it danced with expressions more beautiful than a rainbow in the snow.

I've got my cracks but I'm not in pieces yet.

They treat me as a wolf, but you see me as a lamb.

Through no meaning I ascend to the clouds, caught in a storm of why, I rain on my past so it can no longer reign over me.

They trapped themselves while setting me free.

I began to stretch my hands out further than ever before, I was pulling my arms from my shoulders, I was twisting my fingers backwards across my ribs, hugging myself softly, it was time to acknowledge that while I was alone, I was strong.

So many fights I'll never win but I wait every night to see you again.

All the best art has unavoidable shrapnel.

And as I look out the bus window while I make my way home to an unmade bed, I cry gold tears to an audience of 1000 pink clouds.

My dreams are that my thoughts are worth something to someone else and I know already how much of a fool that makes me.

And I suppose it would be good to be somewhere it never rains, perhaps a summer of love, mosquito nets, no clothes, sunsets and dry nights, watermelon for dinner and cold sided pillows.

I kept plans just for us, I kept thoughts just for you, I am keeping.

We don't move on, we move through. Pain is a maze, and every ending is a version of ourselves that refused to cry.

I move through, full of water, and full of blueberries.

The windows were so big it felt as though if I jumped through them, I would land in a new life, and perhaps I should've jumped. But the vines that laced the edges whispered that they would wrap my ankles if I even tried.

If anything can be made from clouds, then anything can be made from us. For we are clouds with hearts, dance walking through the wideness of our eyes.

Autonomous Sun On The Platypus River

I entered a storm that was so dark and scary, so brutal, cold, lonely, and unwelcome, I closed my eyes at first. With fear swirling I opened them eventually and somehow inside of that storm my vision became clearer than ever. I could see every drop of rain, could taste the smoke from the burning ground from the lightning strikes, I learnt that thunder sings and doesn't roar, I entered a storm that blew me into a new place. This place isn't candy canes and rainbow roads, this place is dark, dry, wastelands, it's still clouds and vultures, wild dogs and ghost gums, I caught seeds in the storm. I filled my pockets with the rain from above and with the seeds of exploded lightning struck pods from the trees below, I'm ready to sow, I'm planting a life under the stars, hoping to grow a sun.

I went downstairs to write; I lay on my bed and made an early entry into the night.

Sleeping in the sun spot, my kaleidoscope eyelids danced like candlelight.

All our promises weren't kept the same, but when I close my eyes it's all okay, I picture us dancing.

I lost the people in which I related to the world from.

All that is left is a pillowcase that tastes of salt, flavoured by pain, damp with tears.

I feel so uncomfortable, almost everywhere.

So, I dream of moving, and thinking I will be comfortable somewhere new.

I'm learning my discomfort is internal and not external, I have to clean inside, I need new furniture inside, I need new scenery inside, then maybe I will be comfortable everywhere once there's an Eames sitting in my lungs.

I'm trying to read but my thoughts are so loud I'm constantly interrupting myself.

There comes a time when we all feel a little broken, when our future no longer predicts warm weather and perfectly cooked toast.

And somehow, I'm supposed to stop loving everyone who stopped loving me.

I believe in me because it was the only job left. But I feel guilty about my survival. I'm afraid to shine, even though I know the world needs my light. I'm afraid to be new, to be changed, I can't help but want to seek permission to be who I want to be. And I can't help but feel as though I will be denied no matter how much light I generate.

Sometimes I just don't want to be.

People look at situations like clouds in the sky. They see what they are told to by the person next to them and so on and so on.

When I am out walking, I try give everyone a smile who looks my way. Just in case they also are crying inside and I do it regardless of the fact my teeth are bad.

Shame is the indentation of your body in your mattress after days of being wrapped in the arms of your own linen. Unwashed, thinking, drinking tea, lighting candles, and still only a few tears.

No one writes or talks about the broken hearts between friends, it's much sadder than lovers, I promise.

When we are lost in the world, we need to create a voice in our heads that remind us that our best, happiest, and most loveable memories are ahead of us. Grieving memories as though they are your last good ones should be left for the montage your head plays when you truly are dying.

Of course, there is no excuse for hurting people, but there are always reasons. And some things hurt less when they are known and understood.

I've moved many times in my life, from varying homes and towns and cities and couches and beaches. Some places have been worse to live in than others, but the worst place to live, the loudest, most excruciatingly heartbroken place I have lived was inside my own head. A place with no rainbows, a loveless wasteland, a place you want to run from, a highway that has no exit, a permanently recurring disappointment. And the thing that makes this place worse than any other is just how many neighbours I have.

# Autonomous Sun On The Platypus River

With loaded guns they wanted a corpse, the vultures are circling in a grey sky above, but the body is moving, the skin regenerates, I'm walking, looking back on a shadow I need to find shade just to escape from, looking towards a horizon that's non-existent.

Writing isn't beautiful, it's disgusting. Our disembowelled thoughts, are an intestine of ugly memories. It makes me sick, and so I will vomit for you all.

My memories are hot chocolate and snow, but they are also a sip of vodka disguised as water.

I would like one thing to last long enough in my life that when it dies so will I.

I see myself there sometimes, on the sand. In the few times I swam in the ocean I really loved it, I felt clean, I felt like how I assumed everyone else felt in the world. Unafraid. Though I never wanted anyone to know, it was my secret that I loved the ocean, and it was well known I hated my body, despite my efforts to blame the big blue of calm and catastrophe I rarely entered. I've never really fooled anyone.

Going outside, shopping, getting coffee, watching a sunset, eating a doughnut, drinking a beer. Sadness, all of it, without you, sadness.

Staying in bed, drinking tea, petting a kitten, eating toast, watching a movie, listening to music. Sadness, all of it, without you, sadness.

Think of us like flowers with lots of petals, but not an infinite amount, some people come to you and water you. Others come to you and pick your petals, some come like the wind, they don't mean to but they are blowing you over taking parts of you with them, and sometimes as flowers we go through so many sets of bad weather or people picking at our petals, we end up just a stem, I know you and me have both been stems in our lives. But to me now, if I was looking out in a field, I'd see you, you'd be a sunflower, tall beautiful and full of petals, and I can see you only because I'm almost a nice tall sunflower myself with more petals than ever before.

There is a child inside me, crying in his bedroom, with sore ribs, and a bleeding nose.

Am I supposed to know everything now? I don't think I am, I don't think I'm supposed to understand it all, no one else does, why me? Why do I even want to, I don't even think I do, the more I understand the less I can handle.

Say no to drugs, if you want, it's ok.

Now that you've left the city, life is a little less exciting, I used to love living in the fear of running into you.

I can't leave my house and I can't leave my head. I'm living inside two places I always run from. Everyone is telling me to clean them, make them places you love, eat better, fix your teeth, make magic.

We could move to a town with a train running through the middle of it. A place where all the signs are selling things that don't exist anymore. With orange sleeves hanging on the clothesline, autumn leaves falling in the sunshine. Would we be happy with no distractions, watching trees be still in the lake, watching birds wondering if today we should bake?

We could move to a town with a train running through the middle of it, raise a couple children have them waving to it. Straight after lunch, ham sandwiches followed by a goodbye to the foreign carriages.

We could stay put, with a siren in our head. There are lovers on the footpaths, hiding behind the bins, no place for the little ones but we love it, we do, me and you.

People who don't know anything about themselves will shout across the rooftops the things they think they know about everyone else.

We made a lifetime of memories, and I'll spend my life remembering them.

The unbearable grieving of loss in my friendships is not because they are dead to me but because I am dead to them.

I guess finding someone to love can be as simple as finding someone who walks at the exact same pace as you and who laughs when you talk.

Books and humans are the same. What's inside of them is all that matters. Some people collect books and never read them, some people collect humans and can't read them. Some don't try. Others take a pen and try to rewrite them. And the worst will open you up with an eraser in their hands, and a blindfold over their eyes.

It isn't love that hurts and breaks us, it's people who don't know how to love that put holes in your heart. And being hurt doesn't make you exempt from hurting others, sadly in many ways it makes you all the more likely to do so.

When a lie becomes the truth, everyone listening gets hurt.

She told me about how she saw the world as the fire cast her into a Coppola film right before my eyes.

There are times in life when you can be in conversations and afford to have your attention drift off, but rarely do those times involve women.

Most days I don't want to do anything, and what's worse is that on the days I do feel like I can do things, there is nothing to do.

If I could make a phone call from the top of this mountain, I'd call all the people who hate me and tell them I will love them all forever.

You look to the sky and ask questions that only the sky can answer.

I want to be there for people the way the sky is, I want to be thought of with the regularity of the sun and the beauty of the moon. I want to warm them in the day and be beautiful at night.

Everyone is engaged in their own private boxing match inside their head and so many are losing that fight.

The ocean shouted my words for me, every night as I went to sleep. It roared me to rest.

And as I walked, winding the button grass plains like a snake, I shed my old skin and left a casing of who I no longer wanted to be on the doorstep of a wombat's burrow.

I took all my sins with me to a small hut off the track and threw them in the fire. I watched as they cried and their tears turned the flames from red to blue. Providing a warmth that spread like love.

As I went to sleep, the hut was singing lullabies.

She was hiding in the cupboard last time I saw her, and before that she was inside a crack on the foot path and the time before that she was on the string of a kite.

I whispered my goodbyes as she sat curled behind the bowls that we only used when we had guests.

We can wait forever for our love.

You won't get anywhere abiding by the rules of art while you make it.

I used to be able to make you feel, in our wildest moments we were amazing. I haven't seen you eat across from me in over a year, I miss looking at you and saying nothing, knowing you can feel me.

This is a book from the future written for the past.

I had no choice but to write. I had no choice but to show the capacity of my love, as my life continues to tick, I fill with more love, love I receive from an infinite source. In the hope it drowns the demons that not only have I collected but that have been forced down my throat and slipped through to my shoulders to carry.

Everyone is so damn obsessed with the sun, soaking their bodies in her rays, searching for beauty in something you can't even look directly at without hurting your eyes.

It's not your responsibility to grovel to people for an acceptance that they didn't give even when they loved you.

Giving up on people when they need you most, is the same as throwing your TV in the bin when the remote needs new batteries.

Do birds ever get so fat they can't fly? Do people ever get so hurt they can't cry?

I have nightmares piling up at the back of my mind, I'm going to crack my skull open, push them out one more time.

I am sleeping in creeks, breeding new dreams. Patting platypus.

I don't want to worry anymore; I want to walk into every room and be confident that someone in it could love me.

I had a big room, with a nice bed, it was full of plants and was filled with golden light each morning from the east facing window. In this room I felt like a dog in a laundry. A pet that was made to sleep outside. A guest in my own house, a stranger in my own world.

Most nights turn into mornings, some mornings god comes pouring through my windows, others he just sits at the ledge tapping on the glass. Smirking as I wake with one eye open and the other half stuck with sleep glued to my eyelids. Some mornings god is in the kitchen making me eggs and chorizo for breakfast. Some mornings I hear his bell ringing on his bike as he cascades down the hill outside my window on the way to the market. One morning in the pouring rain I heard the birds outside arguing over the best way to have a coffee, the birds sat there all pleading their cases one by one as God poured varying product into each of their cups laughing the whole time. The finch liked almond milk, while the magpie liked cow's milk, and the crows preferred their coffee black, the kookaburra mostly drank tea, so he joined god in his laughter. Some morning's I pretended I slept 8 hours.

Perhaps I would love my life as it is today if I were actually living in it today, but I am stuck in yesterday and terrified of tomorrow.  I am in limbo between who I was, and who I want to be, which makes it hard to know who I am.

Pain and guilt had me turning to the truth but I spun in circles looking for it, and looking for you.

No matter how dirty or low the creek gets, it flows.

If you come looking for me you won't find who you remember, you will find who you forgot.

I think sometimes that the whole point of my life is just to be sad, and to figure out what to do about it, so I can tell others. Sometimes it seems as though being broken is what makes me whole, I don't know what I am without disappointment, rejection, anxiety, fear, and yet I survive all of it. I suppose I am supposed to document that, for you, or maybe for me.

It's as though I keep building skyscrapers of my life in a sky full of wrecking balls.

If there are unforgiven people in your life, you must think of them as voodoo dolls for yourself, the more pins you put in them, the more pain you will feel.

I just want to sleep, in the normal hours, with normal people, in a normal bed, and have normal dreams, and normal nightmares.

I want a baby but a baby would not want me.

I live on the tenth floor, sometimes when I look out my window, I see a vision of myself falling from the roof. I see myself quickly getting dressed and running down the stairs, to the very bottom in where I stand with my eyes open and my arms closed.

In another life everyone hugs me goodbye and sends me letters while I'm away, I see God in a bird not a platypus, and my favourite food is avocado with lemon.

I have no reason to fight, and nothing to hide, but my heart has boxing gloves on and my head holds a knife at night.

She told me she can't fix me, but that it was okay for me to love her because she knows that will help me heal.

Is grace for me? Am I worthy of whatever it is that this could be? I guess no one is, but I'm on my knees screaming Allah Akbar and save me Jesus. Looking for a God in the street, looking beside creatures, medicating under a leaking red light, stumbling to a path that makes me feel alright.

And it's so damn unfair that the trees lose their leaves for winter, stripped, and cold, are they afraid? Naked and swaying, I'm just a tree in my mirror this morning.

My favourite thing this year was when I drank my muffin and ate my coffee inside the big window of the cafe and a toy-car-red bus flew by on the road outside and for a second the whole room was blanketed in a sun lit cellophane. For one second everyone inside starred in life's movie, everyone was beautiful. For one second everyone's mouths stretched to the corners of their ears and smiles poured into the floorboards, leaving scuffs of happiness forever.

For one second, I forgot how bad my sleep has been, for one second, I felt only red, for one second, I felt no longer blue.

How am I supposed to let go of something that I carry on the inside, something I am not holding, something pumping through my veins, how do you let go of a love that flows, to your heart, and fills the cracks from past breaks, how I do let go of that, tears? Can I bleed tears?

I went to sleep at 10pm and woke up two hours later after having nightmares from my past. It's like there is a graveyard of memories in my head, and all the ghosts, of all the bad that has been inside of me, despite now being dead, continue to haunt.

I don't want to go back to sleep, I am so afraid of the life I live in my dreams.

I can't help but feel when I finally try to fly, that I will always be dodging bullets in the sky.

Firing squads down below, guns with the names of my dreams on them, fingers on triggers, waving goodbye to future plans.

Will there be enough feathers scattered in the clouds to fill a pillowcase soft enough to dream some more dreams again, or is my life to be forever lost in the wind.

Whenever I see the sky go to a muted pale-blue colour late in the day I'm reminded of the photo I took of you outside our home. You were wearing my coat. And you really looked beautiful man.

Do all the dead leaves of autumn go to heaven? Do all the cats who were hit by cars? Do all the birds who flew into windows, perch on the gates? Do all the dogs who were put down for biting children go to hell? God, I hope not.

I have spent my life in a dark place, it's as though I was born in a cave. I've spent so much of time following tiny lights in the hope of finding big ones. Lights the size of fireflies have guided me, I've chased them, held them, squashed them and lost them. After thirty years even now it's still dark for me, but there is a big glow nearby, I can feel it, I can't see it, but I feel it.

I am no longer cold in winter and I've no longer a use for a double bed or two pillows anymore.

I felt so bad polluting the trees and the creek with my sadness, but I poured into them knowing they are strong enough to hold the mistakes and pain of my life.

We matter about as much as ants do, and ants matter a lot.

Sometimes I think I am just writing to break my fall, hoping to land amongst the words, a place I can try to make sense of it all.

I cut my teeth on books of religion, society, philosophy and history all while crawling on my bedroom floor clinging to the shelves in front of my bed. But I learnt all I know about life from the mountains and the trees. The wind told me secrets the books wouldn't allow to be written, I crawled in the dark, then I walked in the light.

Do I look broken, can they see the damage that's been done, if I was an item in a store would I be discounted, would I be of less value, could they see that I had been opened up, dropped, and no longer work as well as I was designed to?

In the future am I a man who is loved? Loved the way plants love the sun and the way bees love plants and the way we love honey, and the way we make names for those we eat breakfast with. Will I be loved, by me?

There's a tattoo on my heart, burnt into my skin, it hurts to touch. Though when I see my chest in the mirror, I feel good, I feel free. I see a memory of two boys learning how to love everyone but each other and themselves, and themselves, and themselves.

There is a strange green light flickering inside the phone booth beside the empty ranger's cabin. I want to use it but I have no one to call.

.

I want to be told I'm not a bad person but the only person I want to hear it from is never going to speak to me again.

Dear you, turn me into a tiny speck.

Please leave me on the line, don't shrink me in the dryer.

I have a dream where I watch you go and I laugh instead of trip down the well I'm in now.

I can still see the night sky from down here, I can still feel time splashing cups of water on its face as it runs a marathon through the rubble of our history.

I don't know how to love but I'll pretend if it makes you happy and keeps your tinker-bell heart pumping.

And the nothingness is surrounding me and me it, every step I take I apologise for my inconvenience as not all my tears will be caught by my swinging shoe below.

Sorry for the puddles.

I got off the trails and began swimming in the streams, I was freezing, I was scared, I could feel myself growing, so I refused to get out.

I'm happy in my dreams, and sad in my life. I want nightmares. I want sunlight on a rocking chair.

When I closed my eyes, I could see the bear that used to fight everyone in the woods down by the lake eating sourdough with the salmon and ducks.

When I closed my eyes, I could see myself walking into a big room to many cheers and a round of applause, and then moments later that room is hit by an asteroid and there's nothing but desert surrounding me and I'm alone again, wandering, wondering.

Another night where I can't sleep, some soft piano playing out of my phone speakers as I scan my room. I can see the shadows of all I own, hanging in the dull light from the empty streets outside. Cars go by maybe once an hour, like sheet lightning, I am reminded a life is being lived.

I'm a bubble gum boy, pink and pushed out of mouths, swallowed or spat, either way as long as I'm chewed and out of sight my existence is good.

How am I ever going to be sleeping well in a bedroom of hanging shadows.

I'm a bubble gum boy.

And so now that I am dancing, please don't stop me.

Dinner tonight was twelve cinnamon doughnuts.

I will run into this night with sparkles on my shoulders and rockets on my feet. I will see you in heaven, or down at the shops.

And so that's who I am, covered in moss and rocks, drenched in a never-ending supply of water, the autonomous sun, on the platypus river. I'm in there now. I am drinking, dancing, slowly but surely dying, knowing an ocean exists somewhere at the end of this stream and so I shine on, planning my route with the kamonohashi.

Made in the USA
Middletown, DE
30 July 2022

70243085R00149